HOME BUYING
- FOR -
BEGINNERS & DUMMIES

By: Bradley Banks

Copyright © 2019 by Bradley Banks

All rights reserved.

No part of this book may be reproduced in any form or by any electronic or mechanical means including information storage and retrieval systems, without permission in writing from the author. The only exception is by a reviewer, who may quote short excerpts in a review.

Table of Contents

- IMPORTANT DISCLAIMER 4
- INTRODUCTION 5
- CHAPTER 1: GETTING STARTED AND DEFINING GOALS 7
  - WHY YOU NEED A HOME 7
  - OWNING VERSUS RENTING 9
  - QUESTIONS TO ASK YOURSELF BEFORE BUYING A HOUSE 11
  - KEY ACTION STEPS 13
- CHAPTER 2: REAL ESTATE AGENTS 14
- CHAPTER 3: ALL ABOUT HOME INSPECTIONS 30
  - HOW TO USE A HOME INSPECTION REPORT TO SAVE MONEY 32
  - PICKY HOME INSPECTION? 34
  - CAN A HOME INSPECTION HELP YOU SELL YOUR HOME? 36
  - TOO FEW INSPECTIONS 38
  - THE TOP SIX PROBLEMS THAT HOME INSPECTORS FIND 43
- CHAPTER 4: PROS AND CONS OF BUYING A HOME 47
  - PROS 47
  - CONS 49
  - WHAT TO CONSIDER 50
- CHAPTER 5: MAKING AN OFFER 53
  - THE PROCESS 53
  - WHEN USING CASH 54
  - WHEN USING MORTGAGES 55
  - KEY ACTION STEPS 57
- FAQS 58
- CONCLUSION 62

Important Disclaimer

Please note the information contained within this document is for educational and entertainment purposes only. All effort has been executed to present accurate, up to date, and reliable, complete information. No warranties of any kind are declared or implied. Readers acknowledge that the author is not engaging in the rendering of legal, financial, medical, or professional advice. The content within this book has been derived from various sources. Please consult a licensed professional before attempting any techniques outlined in this book.

By reading this document, the reader agrees that under no circumstances is the author responsible for any losses, direct or indirect, which are incurred as a result of the use of the information contained within this document, including, but not limited to, — errors, omissions, or inaccuracies.

Introduction

This book contains proven steps and painless strategies about buying a home.

Buying a home is probably the single largest purchase most people will make in their lifetime. It is a complicated process, and, unfortunately, we all know someone who's suffered from buyer's remorse. Maybe the home didn't really fit their needs, or the location was far from ideal. Perhaps they overpaid, or they bought a lemon that rapidly became a money pit. Whatever the story, the potential for costly and emotionally upsetting problems is what makes home buying so scary for many people.

This book will make you a savvy shopper; one who's less likely to purchase the wrong home and more likely to get the best possible deal for their money. I will take you step by step through the complete home-buying process—from determining if you are ready to buy; to financing, inspections, and negotiating; and finally to closing escrow and enjoying your new home. The book is written in chronological order, breaking the process down into chapters and identifying tips along the way that will save you money and improve your odds of getting the home you want. Of course, markets will vary according to local economies, but whether you're in a seller's or buyer's market, there are steps you can take to improve your bargaining position.

Let's get started!

Chapter 1: Getting Started and Defining Goals

This chapter will focus on the basics of home buying and will get you started on defining your goals. It will give you a roadmap of what you need as well as some ideas of what you need to do when you are feeling overwhelmed. In such kinds of situations, going back to the basics always helps. In this chapter, we will also ask ourselves all the valuable questions and create a guideline for ourselves on what we need to do.

Why You Need a Home
Owning a home has so many benefits, and these include:

1. **Financial savings** - The first and most important one is that you save money. Every month, landlords expect a payment from you when you are renting. They do not care whether you made a lot of money or whether you are doing badly. Having a home ensures that you do not have to worry about rental payments. No one will threaten to evict you because you are late in paying rent, even though owning a home also has its costs after you get the keys.
2. **Profit potential** - The value of a home always appreciates over time, and if the market is

right, you can sell your home for much more than you bought it for. This makes homes such huge assets. Some people buy a home, live in it for a few years, and then sell it for a profit. They then use the extra money to buy their permanent home.
3. **Confidence** - When people own a home, they become more confident in their abilities to even make bigger investments. Couples also become settled mentally because they have a place that they can call home. Owning a home will put you at ease, especially if it is your first home.
4. **Security** - When it comes to security, rental spaces are not always 100% safe. In fact, you are not fully in control of making an impact in terms of security enhancements since that is the landlord's job. Having your own home means you can beef up security as much as you like. Some of these security measures cannot be done in a rental space.
5. **Décor and architecture** - You can customize your home to the design that you have always wanted. You can renovate, use the tiles you like, change the bathroom as much as you want, and essentially bring to life the house of your dreams. It is very exciting to live in a space whose design you love. You cannot carry out major renovations in rentals because it is someone else's property.

6. **House versus home** - Owning a home makes you transform the space from just being a physical structure into being a real home. There is a difference between living in a house that you don't own and a home that you have bought. There is a certain peace of mind that a homeowner enjoys that tenants do not.

Owning versus Renting

Renting a house has its advantages. For example, when you rent a house, you are going to make a smaller financial investment. The owner is in charge of major repairs in the home, and you do not have to worry when the building loses value since you have little to no investment in the building. Renting also means you can move when you like and, in the event of natural disasters, you only bear the loss of your property and not the whole building.

However, owning your home also has more benefits that far outweigh the benefits of renting and leasing. We have covered some of these advantages in the section above, but here are some more benefits for you to think about:

1. **The rent costs outweigh the buying costs** - This is the case in prime apartments. For example, if you stay in a prime apartment in a city like New York for years and you pay high amounts of rent, you may end up spending more money

than you would have buying a house in another city.

2. **You develop financial discipline** - Some home buyers are able to pay the down payment for a house immediately while others need to come up with a payment plan. The second option can discipline you to save more and to even make better financial decisions. These house deposits are very hefty and they may put a hole in your savings, thus forcing you to discipline yourself to earn and save more money. This is a good thing in the long run.

3. **Fewer restrictions** - When renting, there are so many tenancy rules to abide by because the property is not yours. When you own your property, you can do as you please. For example, some apartments have "no pet" policies, and if you are someone who loves pets, this could be a deal-breaker and you may miss out on good apartments. With your own home, this is never an issue.

4. **Privacy** – Most people love their privacy. When renting, you may be living with roommates or neighbors in the same building or area. People are different and not everyone likes the idea of a neighbor knocking on their door any time they feel like it. With homeownership, you can have your privacy and can only talk to neighbors

when you have to or need to. However, this all depends on the personality of the individual; whether they are a private or extroverted person.
5. **No sharing of communal facilities** - You may not be so comfortable sharing facilities with other people. When renting, you may find yourself sharing parking space, a swimming pool, front yard and laundry area. Of course, this depends on the kind of building you live in. With your own home, you have all these facilities for yourself and your family.

Questions to Ask Yourself before Buying a House
Now that we have looked at the reasons why you need to buy your own home, we will look at some of the considerations you have to make. Before the idea of becoming a homeowner crossed your mind and you made the decision to buy a house, there must have been some factors that you weighed on your mind for quite a while.

There are a few questions that you must define and even write down if necessary. The answers you write down in this exercise will guide you in subsequent chapters. Here are some questions to consider:

1. Why? - The first question you must ask yourself is why you are buying the house. Ask yourself the following. Why am I truly buying a

house? Is it something that I truly want? Do I have the means to do it? Is it feasible? Will it improve my life for the better?
2. When? - How soon do you want the house? What is the timeline for the buying process? Will you make all the payments within the required time? How soon do you want to get started?
3. How? - This is the most important step. Some of the questions in this step may only be answered when you get a better understanding of the process. However, there are some questions you can answer immediately. How do you plan to do this? Do you have any experience with home buying? Do you have enough money to cater for this process? Will you be paying with cash or using a mortgage?
4. Where? - Which geographical region do you want to buy a house in? Are you dead-set on living in that area or are you flexible enough to look at other locations? Have you done your research on the cost of houses in that area?
5. What? - What will be the role of the house? Do you want a family home or is it a business asset? Do you know the type/design? Will you live there or will you rent it out? Do you plan to stay in the house for a long time or do you plan to sell it in the near future? What is your budget?

Key Action Steps

Before you move on to the next step, make sure that you:

1. Have defined clearly why you want to own a home.

2. Understand the benefits of buying a home.

3. Are clear on the Why? When? How? Where? and What? questions to ask yourself, and their potential answers.

These are just a few of the key considerations that you have to keep in mind. This chapter has helped to bring things into perspective. You should now be certain that this is what you truly want. You have answered some of the tough questions and are on the right track. This is the first step towards getting your dream home.

Chapter 2: Real Estate Agents

A real estate agent is a person who is licensed to list and sell real estate; a Realtor is a real estate agent who is also a member of the National Association of Realtors. A Realtor is always a real estate agent, but not every real estate agent is a Realtor. In this book, I use the terms "agent" and "Realtor" interchangeably.

People have come to assume that Realtors have no value, especially since the database of homes for sale known as the Multiple Listing Service (MLS) has become accessible to anyone with online access. It doesn't help that Realtors in general rank just below car salesmen in likeability and trustworthiness. However, the truth is that a good real estate agent can save you tens of thousands of dollars and substantially reduce the risks involved with purchasing a home. A bad one can do the opposite, and you'll probably be none the wiser.

Searching the MLS for a home is something you can do on your own. To get inside a house you need an agent. But any monkey can open the door to a house! That's not where the value of a Realtor lies. A Realtor's value lies in his or her knowledge of construction, floor plans, pricing, marketability, finance, hazard insurance, title insurance, surveys, and in their ability to negotiate a great price and protect your rights as a home buyer.

When hiring an agent, it is important that you find a highly-trained, full-time career agent. Your cousin's mother-in-law who sells one or two homes a year may not be qualified to advise and protect you. You want a well-respected, experienced Realtor. Next, you need the right type of representation. The following are the types of agents with which you should be familiar: exclusive buyer agents, buyer agents, dual agents, seller agents, real estate consultants, and discounters. In the following sections, I will describe the roles of these agents.

Exclusive Buyer Agents

An Exclusive Buyer Agent (EBA) works in an office that never takes listings and never represents sellers. Since they represent buyers 100% of the time, there is absolutely no conflict of interest that could jeopardize your negotiating position. To understand the importance of hiring an Exclusive Buyer's Agent, you first need to learn about fiduciary duty.

A fiduciary duty is a legal duty to act solely in another party's interest. It's the same duty that an attorney owes his or her client. When you work with an EBA, they have a legal, fiduciary duty to negotiate on your behalf. Their goal is to help you buy the home of your choice at the lowest possible price and with the best terms. By law, they will owe you the following:

- Loyalty

- Complete confidentiality
- Obedience
- Full disclosure
- Complete accounting for all funds
- Fairness and honesty

Only a single agent (vs. a dual agent) can be fiduciary. You can't have a fiduciary duty to a buyer and a seller at the same time.

Here's the bad news. Less than ½ of 1% of Realtors across the country work as Exclusive Buyer's Agents, and it can be difficult – if not impossible – to find an EBA in some areas. Why? EBAs earn half of what a dual agent earns in any given transaction, so it can be difficult to convince a real estate agent to work only with buyers. It's easier to take a listing, put a sign in the yard, and to wait for an uneducated buyer to come along, pretend they are the buyer's advocate, and sell them the house.

Buyer Agents

Buyer agents work for traditional real estate brokerages that represent both buyers and sellers. There are financial incentives and pressure for these agents to try to sell in-house listings. A Re/Max agent is allowed to sell a Keller Williams listing, for example, but they might get a $500 bonus if they sell a home listed by Re/Max. These types of offices tend to favor the seller far more than the buyer, as evidenced by all the ads telling you how much they have "sold." As a buyer, you are not looking to be "sold," you want to buy without getting ripped off!

You can spot a regular buyer's agent when they ask you to agree – in writing – to "designated agency," "dual agency," or to the use of "intermediaries," discussed below.

Dual Agents/Intermediaries

A dual agent is one that works for the buyer and the seller in the same transaction. It's comparable to a lawyer representing both the husband and the wife in a divorce.

Dual agency is illegal in nearly every other industry, but somehow it continues to exist in the world of real estate. In my view, and in the eyes of most consumer advocates, it's a form of fraud.

Technically, dual agency is not legal in every state, but there is always a way around the law that works against both sellers and buyers, and it's still quite difficult to tell the difference between a "buyer's agent" and a "dual agent," or a "seller's agent" and a "dual agent." Should a Texas Realtor, for example, wish to sell a seller/client's house to one of their buyer/clients, they use a third party in their office to handle negotiations for one of the parties.

This party is called an intermediary. The intermediary's job is to negotiate the price and terms of the real estate transaction without giving advice to either party. Process that information for a moment. From the seller's perspective, they are paying a real estate broker thousands of dollars to sell their home, but their agent can't help them negotiate a higher sales price.

Buyers are on their own with respect to pricing, property condition, and negotiations. The intermediary can give the buyer a list of homes that have sold in the neighborhood, for example, but they can't suggest a fair sales price or write a contract that favors them. They can give them a list of home inspectors, but they won't warn them to walk away from a property due to its condition. The parties are on their own. The Realtors become order takers, and the buyer and seller foot the bill.

The following scenario illustrates what it's like to work with a dual agent or intermediary. Suppose you drive by a house that interests you and notice that there is a Best Realty sign in the yard. You decide to call the number printed on the sign, and a very nice Realtor answers the call.

On the phone, the Realtor offers to show you the house, so you set up a time to meet and view her listing. You like the house but are not ready to commit, so the Realtor offers to show you some other homes that you might like.

In the meantime, they've asked you a lot of questions and have a clear picture of your purchasing power and your level of motivation. If you decide to buy the first house they showed you (or any of their other listings), they'd have to turn you over to someone else in their office (the intermediary), but would still be legally obligated to tell their seller/client everything they know about you.

And, from the seller's standpoint, the agent used their house as a source of buyer leads. The seller most likely shared all of their secrets with this agent, only to have that information used against them if both the buyer side and seller side of the transaction are handled in-house with the same broker. It's a convoluted mess, and it is unfair to both the seller and the buyer; the only person who wins here is the dual agent Realtor and their broker.

Seller Agents

Seller agents work in a traditional real estate office that takes listings or represent sellers. They become dual agents or intermediaries when they represent the buyer. I have yet to meet an agent who only represents sellers; double-dipping by representing both sellers and buyers is very, very lucrative (as are most forms of fraud).

A new trend among Realtors is working within a team, whereby one agent is called the buyer's agent and the other the seller's agent, but don't be fooled. The dual agency scenario still exists in these scenarios. Again, if an agent works for a broker that takes listings, they can't be an exclusive buyer agent. They are a dual agent, transactional agent, or intermediary, no matter what they call themselves.

Real Estate Consultant/Fee For Services

Real estate consultants typically offer services to buyers and sellers on an a la carte basis. For example, instead of paying a 6% commission, a seller can pay a consultant a fixed rate to list the home on the MLS or to provide a market analysis. Buyers can pay an agent a fee to write the purchase contract or to show them a specific home. This is a great way, in my opinion, for real estate to be bought and sold, and more Realtors are beginning to offer these services.

DISCOUNTERS

Most Realtors detest the idea of discounting their commission; I don't. I believe that if a buyer can do much of the legwork, they are entitled to part of the commission. I don't mind working for less money if I can also do less work.

Many discounters are online-only brokers that you never meet, and they never see the house you are buying; they only serve to write the contracts and manage the transaction. My advice is to stay away from these types. If you can find a busy career agent who will reduce his or her commission by offering a reduced level of service, but will still offer you advice and guidance, it can be a great way to buy a house. A really good agent, however, is not going to do the same amount of work for less money. And, as a buyer, it's always a bad idea to put your financial future in the hands of the lowest bidder.

How Agents Get Paid

Real estate commissions are generally a seller's expense (which is why the industry is seller driven). When a homeowner decides to sell their home, they typically hire a traditional Realtor who works with both buyers and sellers. Commissions are negotiable but are typically 5-7 percent of the sale price of the home. The Realtor lists the home on the MLS and, by doing so, agrees to split the commission with the agent who brings a qualified buyer. At closing, the seller's proceeds are reduced in the amount of the negotiated commission. That amount is split between the buyer broker and the listing broker. Agents work under a broker and get paid out of their broker's share of the commission.

To illustrate, let's assume an agent takes a listing on a $200,000 house, and the seller agrees to pay the broker a 6% commission. The house sells for the list price, and the listing broker and the buyer agent's broker each get half of the commission, or $6,000 each ($200,000 sales price x 0.06 commission ÷ 2). The broker shares that $6,000 with their agent.

Some buyers believe that they can get a better price for a home if no Realtor is involved, and at times that's true. The seller might be willing to sell the house for less if they do not have to pay Realtor fees, or they may choose to maximize their own profits. Every transaction and every seller is different.

How To Find A Great Agent

Exclusive Buyer Agents can be hard to find. If you can't find one in your area, you may be forced to work with a traditional agent that represents both buyers and sellers, or who is a self-proclaimed buyer agent. If you're forced to hire a regular buyer agent, don't share too much information with them! You never know when they are going to switch to the other side.

If they have a listing in your price range, they are almost certainly going to show it to you; selling you that home will allow them to earn both sides of the commission. The buyer's negotiating position is highly compromised in this type of office, and a truly level playing field only exists when the buyer works with a single agent. Share what you must but keep some things to yourself, like how much home you can afford, how much cash you have in the bank, and how desperate you are to move out of your apartment.

Treat The Realtor As A Friendly Adversary, Not As Someone You Can Trust With Your Money!

Interviewing Agents

Always meet a prospective agent before you decide to work with them; a phone interview is never enough. The agent/buyer relationship can be a long one, and the two personalities need to "click" to a certain degree. Imagine spending weeks looking at homes with someone you don't like (or who doesn't like you). Here are some questions you need to ask prospective agents:

1. How Long Have You Been In Business?

Because the buyer assumes the risk in a real estate transaction, you need an agent with at least 3-5 years' experience or a new agent that works very closely with their highly skilled broker. The broker and the agent should work as a team.

2. Whom Do You Represent?

Most agents will say that they represent both buyers and sellers, sometimes at the same time. Some will say that even though they work in a traditional real estate office, they only work with buyers, or that they are their office's buyer specialist. The truth is that it doesn't matter what they say; if they are not an Exclusive Buyer's agent, they represent both sides. It is imperative that I make this point clear.

Most states now require that a Realtor discloses whom they represent at your first "substantive" meeting, usually in writing. This is your opportunity to discuss this important issue in greater detail.

3. How Do You Handle Competing Buyers?

What happens if the agent has a buyer who is looking for the same type of house as one of their other buyers? Who gets the first look at the property, and what happens if both buyers want to make an offer?

My personal policy is that I won't represent two clients looking for exactly the same property.

4. How Do You Handle In-House Listings?

There are incentives for Re/Max agents, for example, to show Re/Max listed homes. How will they handle this conflict of interest? How do they handle representing both the buyer and seller in the same transaction? Are you going to be turned over to another agent to handle your negotiations? It's imperative that you know and understand their procedures, and don't let them convince you that it's not a big deal. It is.

5. How Will You Notify Me Of New Listings?

Most offices have some kind of auto-search capability, which automatically sends new listings to their clients the moment they are entered in the MLS. Buyers can go online and look at pictures, take virtual tours, and make notes about the homes they like. It helps all parties to communicate about specific homes and to stay organized.

6. How Much Notice Do You Need For Showings?

A successful career agent isn't going to be available at the drop of a hat to show you a home. I schedule my weekend showings three to five days in advance but I am often more flexible during the week. In a swift-moving seller's market, it's often necessary to act quickly and I do my best to make myself available.

I have an assistant who can show a home for me in case of a scheduling conflict. Find out how your prospective agent works.

7. How Do You Get Paid?

Commissions are negotiable, but many residential buyer agents work for 3% of the sales price; the fee is deducted from the seller's proceeds at closing. Some Realtors charge buyers an upfront retainer, which is fully refundable at closing. Realtors often use retainers to eliminate buyers who are time wasters. I sometimes collect a small, refundable deposit ($100), but there are many agents who will be inexperienced or desperate enough to drive you around and show you houses for free. Others want their gas money upfront.

8. Can I Review Copies Of Your Paperwork?

Don't feel pressured into signing a buyer's representation agreement on the spot. Take it home, review it, and negotiate the terms with which you don't agree.

9. What Happens To Bonuses That Are Offered To The Selling Agent?

It's not uncommon for builders and sellers to offer sales incentives to the agent who brings them a qualified buyer, and more often than not the buyer is completely unaware until it's too late to object. Find out the policy of the agents you interview. Some agents will state that they can keep the bonus as long as it is disclosed to all parties. Don't hire this agent! You must be able to trust that the advice they give you is independent of any additional financial incentive. My policy is to rebate all bonuses and money in excess of the negotiated commission back to the buyer. That should be your expectation as well.

10. What Happens If The Seller Only Offers 2% To The Buyer's Agent, But Your Agent Works For 3%?

This happens sometimes with bank-owned properties or sellers who have little equity in their home. Are you willing to pay your agent the extra one percent by rolling it into the price of the home? Will you pay the agent in cash? If not, do you want your agent to even show you homes that offer less than a three percent commission? This is an important issue and you would do well to make your wishes known.

Meaningless Questions

You can ask the following questions if you like, but don't put too much stock in their answers.

1. Do You Have References?

All agents have references, but it doesn't necessarily mean those references are meaningful or even real. Visit the real estate commission in your state to see if they have been disciplined for any reason. Get a referral from a friend if you can, but always have an exit strategy or a plan to end the relationship if it is not working out.

2. Can You Give Me A List Of Buyer Clients With Their Addresses And How Much They Saved?

An agent who would give you this information is not very smart. I would never compromise my client's safety and privacy in order to get a new client. New homeowners become the target of many, many scams, and I'm not going to inadvertently become part of a transaction that harms my clients. Find an agent who has integrity and concern for things other than their own pocketbook.

3. How Much Of A Discount Can You Usually Get Off The Price Of A Home?

There are far too many variables for anyone to be able to answer this question accurately, and any answer you receive would be a complete guess or a lie. Price is only one of many possible seller concessions. If five buyers are competing for the same house, for example, you want the agent that is going to be able to convince the seller's side to sell the house to you, not one of the other four buyers. You need an agent who can present your offer in a way that wins you the house, and often it has nothing to do with money.

Buyer Representation Agreements

A buyer's representation agreement is an employment contract that spells out the duties and responsibilities of the Realtor to the buyer, and vice versa. Most Realtors will want you to sign one. In fact, some won't show you a home until they have you under contract. Realtors want to ensure they will be paid for the work that they do, and it is unfair for a buyer to use their services to tour houses only to switch Realtors or buy the home through a discounter at the last minute.

The problem with buyer rep agreements is that they provide far more protection for the broker than for the buyer. There is nothing that guarantees client satisfaction or that protects you from an unskilled or unethical agent. It doesn't list their duties or discuss their responsibilities toward you even though it demands your loyalty to the brokerage for an extended period of time.

Don't be afraid to negotiate and dictate the terms of this agreement. Here are some ways you can tweak your contract with your agent if you must sign one:

- Instead of committing to a six-month agreement, adopt a one-month agreement with an option to renew at a later time. This will give you some time to get to know your agent before making a long-term commitment to them.
- Have the commitment apply only to the houses that they show you, and omit any mention of a time period.
- Designate a trial period, after which the full agreement goes into effect unless either party terminates the agreement.

- Most importantly, always insist on an "out" clause so that you can be released at any time. The agent will only be paid on homes that they have shown you, should you choose to buy one of those homes. A good agent is going to have some sort of customer satisfaction guarantee. If they don't, find someone else.

I personally don't use this type of buyer's representation agreement. In fact, I don't even ask a buyer to sign one. I'm confident in my skills. If a buyer/client doesn't want to work with me, they are free to go at any time with no strings attached. Working with me should be the least stressful part of the homebuying process. It's not unreasonable for you to expect the same from the agent you hire.

Chapter 3: All About Home Inspections

Getting the Most Out of Your Home Inspection

You've located the home of your dreams. Your real estate agent has drawn up the offer and the offer has been accepted. Now you have a few weeks in which to perform your due diligence – your research on the home. Is this home everything you think it is? When your agent asks you if you want to get a home inspection, your answer should be "Yes." Following the six tips here will maximize your home inspection results.

Get the best inspector. A really good inspector will catch just about every problem that exists in a home, and be able to put the issues into perspective for you so that you can make a decision. Your inspector should be licensed and/or certified at what they do, and have a good experience level. Your agent will give you several names; either call each one or research them on the internet. The best inspector and the worst inspector will likely charge you the same amount of money, so why not maximize your return?

Be there for the inspection. 85% of home buyers are not present during the inspection, thinking that they will disturb the work of the inspector. Not so. The inspector will welcome you for the inspection, and be glad that they can point out the most important issues to you so that you fully understand what he/she has found.

Ask the right questions. Your inspector is making value judgments as they inspect – would they buy it? Ask your inspector to be honest with you – take advantage of this special "inspector-client privilege" relationship to ask him/her what their concerns are. These are things they won't write in the report, but they will discuss it with you.

Ask for a "show and tell" on any items you do not understand. If you are not at the home during the inspection, arrange for a call with your inspector after the inspection to discuss these items. The inspector will tell you things over the phone that may not be in the report.

Maintenance advice. Although not part of the formal inspection, most good inspectors will tell you what items in the home require regular maintenance and will tell you what that maintenance consists of. Take advantage of the inspector's expertise.

Ask for referrals. Who does the inspector recommend for repairs? This is also something you will not see in the formal report, but the inspector will have a few very talented tradespeople that they use and you should find out who these people are.

Follow these tips to get the most out of your due diligence. Buying a home is one of the largest investments you will make; don't put yourself in the position of finding serious problems after the sale and being trapped. This up-front effort will ensure you know exactly what you are getting.

How To Use a Home Inspection Report To Save Money

Should you use a home inspection report to make a home buying decision? Definitely. Realize that I am biased in favor of this advice because I was once a home inspector. The stuff I found on inspections was a constant source of surprise to me. All homes have defects. While most are minor, all it takes is one big one to blow the budget over to the next county.

I am also an airplane nut. This summer at an airshow, I held a talk about building your own airplane. Afterward, someone came up to me and said they were going to purchase a used homebuilt aircraft that very day. I asked them who they were having inspect the craft before the purchase. They said that they were skipping the inspection, saying, "It flew in here to the show so it must be fine."

If you're buying a house, this is like saying the home's roof doesn't leak water so everything must be fine inside.

Whether you are buying an airplane or a home, get an inspection. The price you pay will pale in comparison to what you might end up spending to correct major defects. Here's how to use an inspection report to save you money.

Don't worry about the small stuff. A stuck window can be fixed. A leaky faucet can be repaired. Missing attic insulation can be added. You can even ask the seller to make repairs. They don't have to, but many times sellers will bend over backwards to make you happy. Skip over the small stuff in the report and go to the section called Major Items. These are at the top of the list in the report and/or in the summary.

The seller is supposed to tell you about significant defects. This rarely happens. This is not necessarily because the seller is covering it up, but because they don't know about it. I have gone into dozens of basements to find furnaces that were recalled because of carbon monoxide hazards and the owner had no idea (and was lucky).

A note about inspectors. Inspectors are picky, especially new ones. Real estate agents know this and it drives them crazy. Agents want you to be happy with your new home as much as you do, and they have to wade through the small stuff too. As long as you pick an experienced and unbiased inspector, pay attention to the major items and if you find something concerning, get an opinion on the cost to correct the fault.

The significant items that you want to focus on are the things that will either hit your wallet in a big way or will be a risk to your safety and well-being in the home. The maintenance and repair items are handy to have, but every home has an assortment of them.

A few final points. The first is that there is no requirement to do anything with a home inspection report. The report contains the advice of a qualified and experienced inspector so that the seller and buyer can determine the condition of the home and head off unanticipated surprises. The second point is to rely on your real estate agent for perspective. They have done this many times, and as a professional will nearly always give you accurate and thoughtful advice.

Picky Home Inspection?
I recommend a home inspection for sellers as well as buyers. By obtaining a home inspection, sellers can find out ahead of time what the inspector will identify as a problem. Buyers can find out if there are any money traps in the home and get a good idea of a home's general condition.

Readers have asked me some thorny questions over the years about "picky" home inspections, and how to differentiate the little things from the big things. I'll try to answer that question here.

The point of a home inspection is to find the big things that would introduce financial hardship for the buyer that they would otherwise not know about. This includes structural defects, plumbing errors, architectural or builder errors, electrical defects, or lack of maintenance that has compromised any of the major systems in the home.

Home inspections are not specifically designed to catch code violations, although an inspection should point out safety deficiencies. An example is an older home where a bedroom has been added where there is no window in the room. An inspector will flag this condition not specifically because it violates the code for a "sleeping room," but because it is a safety issue. In the event of a fire in the hall, where will the person sleeping in this room escape to? So, "no window" could be a serious problem if the buyers were to assume this room was a bedroom.

Other minor safety issues may be called out on the report but are usually not loaded into the "significant" category. These issues are, for example, the spacing between pickets on a deck rail. If the home was built prior to the code going into effect, then there is no violation. While the inspector can list this type of item in his/her report, there is no obligation on anyone's part to correct them. "Picky" report items are usually those items that do not have relevance given the date the home was constructed and do not pose a substantial safety or structural hazard. If you encounter items like this on the report, you should clarify their significance with the inspector.

As long as you are willing to push the inspector a little on identifying the major issues clearly in the report, then the pickier the inspection the better. As a seller, you will have a good idea of what will turn up on the next inspection, and you'll have a checklist of items to correct. As a buyer, you'll need to wade through the little stuff to get to the major items, but a picky inspection will not be a problem as long as you get clear explanations.

A final note on pickiness. If the inspector is inexperienced (less than 2 years inspecting), they will be very picky because they don't want to miss anything. This could be to your advantage. If the inspector has been inspecting for a long time, then they may not be able to differentiate what is major and what is not. As long as they capture the "big stuff," pickiness should not be a drawback.

Can a Home Inspection Help You Sell Your Home?
Are you trying to sell your home? Buying and selling has picked up here in the mountains, so the difficulty of selling is going down. This doesn't mean that selling your home is easy. It's not. And it can be stressful at every stage.

Will getting a home inspection help you sell your house? Of course, I'm biased, as a former home inspector. But I know that sellers can obtain a big sales advantage by having a pre-sale inspection conducted. Here are the pros and cons.

Getting a seller's home inspection is a good idea if:

- You want to avoid the last-minute surprises of a buyer's home inspection. Sometimes both parties are very surprised at what is found in an inspection. Suddenly there is work, aggravation, and a small measure of irrationality thrown in as both parties wrestle with who will do what. Sometimes unanticipated discoveries will sink the deal. If you have the chance to address these

beforehand, you are more likely to keep the sale.
- If you want an extra edge in marketing the home. Any extra effort or component to make the home more appealing to buyers will help set your home apart from everyone else. Getting an inspection indicates to the potential buyers that you are serious about taking care of the home and selling it with all issues disclosed.
- The home is already in good condition. A home inspection will probably turn up some items that you are unaware of. They will be small items and you can take care of them relatively easily. The inspection report then becomes a marketing tool.
- On the other hand, getting a seller's home inspection may not be a good idea if:
- You know that there are numerous problems with the home and would rather not dig up the details on them. This is a little ostrich-like, but some sellers feel that it is better to not disclose defects and rely on the "buyer beware" doctrine even though they know there may be ramifications at contract due diligence time.
- The home has very serious known defects and is being sold as-is. There is little point in illustrating the multiple deficiencies of a home as a seller in an inspection report when you know the buyer will probably be ordering their own inspection.

- If you are asking a high price for the home and sticking to it. You know the buyer will be getting an inspection but you have already decided not to negotiate. Although risky, this tactic may still bring a buyer as the market picks up but extends the time that the home is on the market.

Most home inspectors offer substantial discounts for seller inspections, and it is typical for the inspection to also include a return follow-up with an updated report. Getting a seller's home inspection can give you a substantial advantage in selling your home for the best price and can reduce the amount of stress that selling a home induces. You will have all of the knowledge without any of the surprises.

Too Few Inspections
With real estate markets picking up, many people have decided to build the home of their dreams. From a small cabin to a large timber frame home, getting the construction details right is critical. As long as you pick a top-quality builder, everything will be fine, right?

Wrong. Even building your dream home from a purchased set of plans will bring errors and omissions. This is the nature of homebuilding. One homeowner I talked to recently said, "It doesn't seem to matter how many homes you build; you think that each one is going to be perfect, and then you discover after you move in that you or someone else forgot something." This is especially true when building the dream home you drew out on a napkin one night over dinner.

If you are building or planning to build, a home from plans or a custom home that has never taken shape before, I have some advice that will save you some heartache. You will have enough surprises even with the best planning.

Get your own inspector. Hiring a home inspector or qualified independent project GC to look at your home at each stage of construction will insure that you get the best possible results.

Why would you want to spend this money? What could possibly go wrong?

On one inspection, I discovered that the electrician had drilled six 2 inch holes through two major roof trusses (a big no-no). Result if not corrected: potential roof/gable collapse.

Installers forgot to flash 4 of the rear windows. Result if not corrected: massive water leaks into the home (tough to correct after siding is on).

I inspected a spec home for sale where the outside deck was not supported properly. I flagged it as unsafe. Before corrections were made a windstorm caused the entire structure to collapse.

On one new home, the contractor forgot to install a drainage system before backfilling the basement walls. Result: a 2-foot-deep swimming pool in the basement.

This is a fraction of what I used to see when I was inspecting. This is not to cast blame on contractors. The majority of builders are highly conscientious, and our municipal inspectors are excellent. However, there is only so much you can manage without having another fresh and educated set of eyes to catch problems. A home is a complicated assembly of systems.

If you go this route, hire your inspector early in the process. When you contract with your builder, tell them that you have an independent inspector and that they will not get in the way. The person you hire will be your advocate, communicating with you so that you can communicate corrections to the builder in time. Your builder may not like this, because they will think you are second-guessing them. But the home is yours, and you want and deserve the best.

Negotiate pricing with your inspector, but expect to pay about $150 per visit. 5-8 inspections are typical. I guarantee that these inspections will end up saving you money on overages and mistakes. There's even a chance you will get into the home and say, "We didn't miss a thing!"

Top Six Myths About Home Inspections

If you have bought or sold a home, you might have experienced an independent home inspection. This type of home inspection is designed to provide both buyers and sellers with critical information about the health of the home's systems – heating and cooling, electrical, plumbing, water tightness, roof condition, and safety. This type of inspection is highly detailed and provides a wealth of information on the home. While this type of inspection is not required, it can help buyers avoid a "money pit" and can help sellers understand what things might turn buyers away.

A reader wrote to me last week to say that they recently bought a house and expected the home inspector to look for termites. After they moved in, they decided to remodel. They discovered that termites had completely eaten the wood structure in 3 walls.

I told them that one of the things home inspectors do not do is inspect for pests since they are not qualified to identify them. Pest control professionals are qualified to find pest infestations and should be called in before the purchase. Most of the time your real estate agent will suggest what inspections you should be getting to protect yourself.

This got me thinking about home inspection myths. Here are the top 6 myths you should know about.

Home inspectors inspect for termites. Myth! Unfortunately for the couple above who believed this, repairs were very expensive.

You should not attend the inspection of the home you are buying, because it will disturb the inspector. Myth! Inspectors appreciate their clients attending the inspection and know they can fully communicate the issues with them. Sometimes written reports do not explain everything fully. If the clients are out of town and cannot attend the inspection, they should hold a conference call to discuss report items as soon as practical after the report is completed.

The seller is responsible for fixing everything the inspector finds wrong. Myth! Repairs, even serious ones, are negotiable. The sellers may be able to back out of a deal, however, if the inspector discovers serious defects.

New construction requires an independent home inspection to get the Certificate of Occupancy. Myth! New construction does require progressive inspections by the municipal building inspector for safety and code enforcement. If you are moving into a newly constructed home, I personally would recommend an independent home inspection also, as it will catch many loose ends.

If the home's appraisal is excellent, there can't be anything wrong with the home and you don't need another inspection. Myth! A home's appraisal is based on many factors, including market conditions, location, and materials (HardiePlank and granite counter-tops, for example) but does not inspect for systems actually working or structural integrity.

A home inspection will take about 30 minutes. Myth! A thorough home inspection should take from 2-5 hours depending upon the size and complexity of the home. There are hundreds of inspection points on a home inspection, including walking the roof and crawling the crawlspace.

Now that you are the home inspection expert, you can try these questions on your friends and see how they do.

The Top Six Problems that Home Inspectors Find
Progress readers routinely ask me what the most common problems are that home inspectors find. If you are buying a home, these issues may cause problems for the sale. If you are selling a home, review these to minimize surprises. You may want to hire a home inspector prior to listing your home if you are aware of any of these issues with your home.

> ➢ Outside grading. Over 60% of the homes I inspected did not have a steep enough slope, or grade, to lead water away in a heavy rain. If you wonder why you have a damp basement or crawlspace – this could be part of the reason. The first 10 feet out from your foundation should drop at least six inches. This may not be easy to do here in the mountains where we build on the side of a hill. What to do: install a drainage ditch on the upslope to lead water away from your home.

- Missing, improperly placed, or damaged gutters. Closely associated with the grading problem above, gutters that are not functioning will introduce moisture into walls, basements, and crawlspaces. Mildew and mold follow, causing damage to materials, and potentially adding contaminants into the air that you breathe. What to do: Inspect your gutters and downspouts both spring and fall and make repairs. Observe what is happening in a heavy rain – your gutters may not be sized correctly. Go out and look – are the gutters carrying away ALL of the water?
- Heating system problems. This is a serious category with health and safety impact. And it's a large category, covering everything from gas leaks to heat exchanger cracks to wood-burning fireplaces that have never been cleaned. I found furnace filters that had not been changed in years, and piles of construction debris still lying inside air supply vents. What to do: Have your heating and cooling system serviced twice a year by a professional. Have a maintenance checklist for the other items (filter schedule for example) and follow it.

- Missing smoke detectors. 65% of the homes I inspected either did not have any working smoke detectors, did not have enough smoke detectors, or the detectors were not in the right places. What to do: check your home now. How many detectors do you have? Are they working? You can push the "test" button on each unit to see if it's working. Buy photoelectric versions if you need more. Install smoke alarms in every bedroom, outside every bedroom, and on every level of your home.
- Undersized or faulty electrical systems. In older homes where small electrical panels (less than 200A) were common, I would routinely see where residents had augmented the outlets with extension cords and multipliers. I would also discover additional distribution panels that had been installed improperly. What to do: Minimize the use of extension cords and multiplex outlets. If you see lots of this in a house you are buying, get an electrician or home inspector to check it out.
- Expired roof materials and cracked plumbing stack gaskets. Asphalt shingle roofs have a life of 15 to 30 years depending upon quality and material. Typically, homeowners move in and

forget the roof unless they suffer a leak. What to do: Hire a home inspector or handyperson to inspect your roof every 3 - 5 years.

Consider starting and keeping a maintenance checklist for your home if you are not already doing it. Why court surprises?

Chapter 4: Pros and Cons of Buying A Home

Pros

- Stability. One of the biggest drawbacks to renting is the uncertainty of not knowing how long you will be able to stay in one location. When you rent, where you live and for how long is at the whim of your landlord or property manager. When you own your own single-family home or condo, so long as you pay your mortgage, it is unlikely that any outside party can force you to move.
- Predictable payments. If you purchase a home with a fixed-rate mortgage, your monthly payment will not change, whereas monthly rents can change annually or even monthly, depending on your contract. Knowing that your housing expense is fixed makes it much easier to plan for other purchases, such as vacations and cars.

Mortgage interest and property taxes paid are tax-deductible. These added deductions can represent a significant tax savings that you don't have if paying rent.

- Building equity. With the economy back on more stable ground, we have seen significant appreciation in property values over the past few years. Although the pace has slowed a bit, home values are still increasing, which means that as values increase, and as you pay down your principal, you are creating equity that you can tap into for college, retirement, or for buying a step-up home in the future.

This is a strong argument for homeownership. Right now, the average rent in San Diego County for a decent two-bedroom condo is around $1650. That is $19,800 a year, and in just five years, that adds up to $99,000! Nearly $100,000 and nothing to show for it.

- Investment opportunity. Depending on the price and monthly expenses, it might be that the first home you buy can later be rented out, allowing you to derive rental income. Now you're the landlord! Many first-time buyers often purchase a more modest first home with this strategy in mind.
- Putting down roots. One of the less obvious benefits of homeownership is people often feel more connected to a community when they own a home in a specific area, and they're more likely to participate or volunteer in local activities or groups.
- Decorate as you desire. Another drawback to renting is the lack of freedom to make your own decorating decisions when it comes to painting, wallpaper, or even updating faucets and light fixtures. When you own your home, you can let the DIY decorator in you run free!

Cons
- It takes money. Lots of money. While there are some loan programs (VA and some credit unions) that require zero down, generally you need at least 3.5% of the purchase price as a down payment for an FHA loan. Conventional loans require 5–20%. That is a lot of money for many people to save.

There are some down payment assistance programs available, and often a seller will help with closing costs. Alternately, buyers often borrow from their retirement accounts or get gift funds from a family member. If you decide to buy, obtaining a pre-approval for a loan will be your first step before looking at homes! Knowing what you can honestly afford will save you disappointment down the road.

You might have to give up some things. Let's say you want to buy a home for $425,000 with an FHA loan. You put down $14,875. With your upfront mortgage insurance premium written into the loan, your loan amount is $417,302. Your monthly payment—including principal, interest, mortgage insurance, taxes, and homeowner's insurance—will be roughly $2,946.00. Depending on where you are purchasing, a single-family home priced at $425,000 might not have a remodeled kitchen or bathrooms, and it is likely you will have to make some cuts in other expenditures, such as entertainment, in order to afford the home.

- If it breaks, you fix it. The nice part about renting is that if the water heater bursts, not only is the owner responsible for replacing or repairing it, but they also have to clean up any mess or damage. You own it, you fix it. This can come as quite a shock to new homeowners, and it is recommended that you have some funds in reserve to cope with unexpected repairs or appliances that need to be replaced. The number of reserves will vary, but lenders often recommend that homeowners have six months PITI (Principal, Interest, Taxes, and Insurance) saved to cover unexpected repairs or loss of income. Not everything is covered by insurance or home warranties.
- Ongoing maintenance. Owning a home or condo has varying levels of maintenance that must be taken care of in order to protect your investment. If you have a single-family home with a yard, you will have regular maintenance, or you'll need to hire a gardener. There will also be numerous other ongoing projects, like cleaning the rain gutters or pest control. On the other hand, if you purchase a condo, expect to pay an average of $280-$400 a month in homeowners' association (HOA) fees to cover maintenance for the complex.

What to Consider

Here are some statements to consider that will help you determine if you are ready to be a homeowner, and if so, whether you would be more comfortable in a condo or single-family home.

1. I like where I live and haven't given much thought to buying.

2. I really enjoy having a swimming pool and gym where I live.

3. I have a steady job and have managed to save some money.

4. I hate the idea of paying rent and having nothing to show for it.

5. I like the idea of moving from city to city to see more of the country.

6. I pay a lot in taxes and would like to have some additional deductions.

7. I consider myself handy and enjoy getting my hands dirty.

8. I don't spend much time at home on evenings or weekends.

9. I'd like to have a place for my kids and/or dog to play outdoors.

10. I honestly don't get bored watching HGTV or DIY Channel.

11. I'm okay with cutting back on dinners out and entertainment to pay a mortgage.

12.   I like knowing that I don't have to move unless I want to.

Don't buy unless you're ready, and make sure you purchase the type of property best suited for who you are and how you like to live—it's a big commitment.

If you're tired of moving and looking for some stability, and if you have a steady, reliable income, you might be ready to buy—at least psychologically. If you're handy, enjoy DIY projects, and want some outdoor space, a single-family home might be your best buy. On the other hand, if you like amenities, such as a pool and fitness room, and are not interested in the responsibility of ongoing maintenance, a condo would probably be more suitable. If you don't mind moving every couple of years and would rather spend your money on travel and/or entertainment or cars, you're probably not a good candidate for buying at this time.

Chapter 5: Making an Offer

So, you have found a house you like and you have fallen in love with the place. Now what? What is the process you need to go through to make it yours? In this chapter, you will learn the process of making an offer and ultimately closing the deal.

The Process
The process of making an offer is different for buyers using cash and those using mortgages. Making an offer also differs from region to region. Different countries or states have their own specifications. Normally, a seller gives the price that they want for the house. They can list it online or give it to your agent. This price depends on the other house prices in the area. However, the price will differ depending on the value of the house, materials, size and other factors that the seller should openly disclose.

You should never offer to pay the seller the exact price he is asking for. You should always bid a little lower. In general, the demand and supply rules apply here. Sometimes, a seller may tell you that the house is in demand to get you to agree to a high price. Occasionally, sellers even hire people to pretend to be buyers so that you can think that the demand is higher than it actually is. Real estate agents and sellers have many tactics that you should be wary of, so during this process, go with your gut.

When you decide to make an offer, your agent will give you some paperwork and you will present this to the seller or their agent. Your offer will include the amount you intend to pay and how you plan to pay for it. The seller may decide to counter the offer or reject it. He may also decide to accept it. Counteroffers are more like negotiations because the buyer and the seller may have different figures in mind. They then have to come to an agreement. No one has an upper hand because they both need each other.

The process of making an offer and finally closing the deal may vary depending on how you intend to pay. For mortgages, more paperwork is involved simply because this is a complicated process. However, for cash, payment can be made once or in two installments, depending on the agreement between the buyer and the seller.

When Using Cash
When paying with cash, you first need to make an offer. Find the house that you want and let the owner know that you want to buy with cash. If you are using a buyer's agent, let them know. Most sellers love cash buyers because the process is faster and secure. Sellers prefer cash over a loan that may not even be approved.

The best thing about paying with cash is you can even negotiate a lower price and the seller may be willing to adjust. Once you and the seller arrive at a good price, you need to inspect the house again. You can get a professional home inspector to do the inspection to ensure that everything is fine. A lot could have changed from the first viewing to the buying time, so wait for the inspector to give you the green light.

If you discover that the house has problems, this is a red flag, and you should walk away from the deal if it is not something you can fix. However, this step all depends on your contract. If you find problems, you can renegotiate and take it for a lower price.

The next step is the appraisal process, where you want to confirm that the house is of the value that you are spending your money on. Do not skip this process. You do not want to realize later that you spent too much money on a house.

After the appraisal process, you need to arrange for insurance. Look for a company in your area that gives good home insurance. The last and most important step is closing the deal and paying the money. When you are arranging with the seller and your agent, you will have a possible closing date. All you have to do is sign the papers and give a check to the seller.

When Using Mortgages
After you find a place you like, you can notify the seller. If a seller accepts that you can pay with a mortgage, you can now get the contract. Review the

contract for a few days before you sign it and ensure that you understand everything. Make sure you have read the contingencies so that you are protected in the event that the deal goes south. I am not saying that this will happen, but it always good to be prepared.

The mortgage process involves a lot of paperwork, so you should ask for the documents beforehand to allow you to go through them in detail. Some of the documents you need are a settlement statement and mortgage letters.

The same way you would do if you were spending cash, inspect the house with a home inspector and look for defects. If you find something wrong with the house, you can negotiate with the seller to reduce the cost. Examine the house for mold, pests, or unstable foundations.

If the house looks fine, it is time to move to the next step. Now you have to write the mortgage application. Look at the costs and read the fine print. Since you already knew what you need, by now you should qualify and should be submitting your application. If you feel like you need to check one last time, go and inspect the house again to ensure there are no issues. Once you sign on the dotted line, there is no turning back.

Finally, double-check and transfer the money to the correct account. After signing and clearing all the paperwork, you will get the keys to the house. Congratulations. You now have your first home!

Key Action Steps

Before you move on to the next step, make sure that you:

1. Make an offer that is lower than the seller's asking price.
2. Get a home inspector to check the house for any potential repair work.
3. Read every document carefully before signing.
4. Send the money to the correct account.
5. Receive all the paperwork for transferring ownership of the house.

FAQs

I have never purchased a home. Where do I start?

The best place to begin is by figuring out how much you can afford. Within your budget, determine the loan amount you feel comfortable paying each month. Next, meet with a lender to get pre-approved. Then start following the Step-by-Step Checklist we've provided.

Does it cost me anything as a buyer to use a real estate agent?

No, typically the commissions for both real estate agents are covered by the seller of the home. That's one of the reasons we highly recommend you use an agent. Why not get all of his/her help if there's no cost to you? Pretty sweet, huh?

How can I find a great real estate agent?

Here are a couple of tips:

- Ask for suggestions from friends and family members you trust. They can tell you a lot.
- If you know the real estate agent's name, type it in Google and read his/her reviews.
- We suggest that you look at a few homes with an agent before you sign an agreement for him/her to serve as your agent. You'll have a better feel of his/her style and approach.

- Want some help? We provide a free service to help you find excellent agents in your area. We'll track down 2-3 excellent agents that get high recommendations. You can then contact the agents and select one that fits with your style.

How long does it take to buy a home?

It varies, depending upon the market. We've worked with buyers who have found their home on the first day out. Others have taken 3-4 months to find what they were looking for. Once you've signed a contract to purchase a home, it will take approximately 30 days from signing the contract to signing the final documents.

Does it cost me anything to meet with a lender and apply for a loan?

The requirements for each bank and lender vary. Some charge you an application fee. Others charge you for the credit report. To apply for a loan, you can pay anywhere from $0-$500.

How do I get the best interest rate?

You have to be careful here. Get a rate quote from several lenders. And ask them to explain the numbers. Putting more money down and having a credit score above 760 will help also.

Should I get my loan from a bank or a mortgage broker?

Talk to both. Choose whoever gives you the best rate with the lowest closing costs. Good insights are given in the Definite Do's section.

How can I spot poor workmanship in a home?

In our experience, most people focus more on the flooring than on the walls and ceilings when they tour a home. Flooring is LOTS easier to replace than poor construction and workmanship. As you walk through a home, look at the quality of workmanship. What is the condition of the paint and sheetrock? Is the concrete damaged? Are the ceilings cracked? Are the windows old and single-paned? If your agent can't help you spot these things, we'd encourage finding an agent who can.

How many homes should I walk through before deciding?

We've worked with clients who initially thought they wanted "this" from a home. But after visiting five or six homes, they realized they wanted "that." Your Wish List could "morph" after touring several homes. That's why we suggest checking out between five and ten homes before you lock in on one. Of course, you could always "stumble" onto an amazing home on the first round and love it.

What does a home inspector do?

The home inspection consists of a visual inspection and a written/electronic report of your property from top to bottom, including all the main systems (electrical, plumbing, furnace, AC, etc.). Some state laws and professional associations require home inspectors to give clients two documents as a matter of business and ethics: written home inspector contracts and written inspection reports. Request both from your inspector.

What is earnest money? And how much is needed?

Earnest money is used to show the seller that you are qualified and serious about buying the home. Depending upon the market and your location the earnest money can be from 1% to 3% of the home's purchase price. (Your agent will counsel you on this). That amount can climb higher in a competitive market. The money will likely be deposited in the escrow account of the seller's broker. That money will go toward the purchase of the home. You can lose your earnest money if you do not meet the deadlines specified in the contract. One of your agent's responsibilities is to keep you on task and safe from losing your earnest money.

Conclusion

Homeownership is one of the most critical parts of life. It could be a rite of passage, a family benchmark, or a dream come true. Whatever the motivation to buy, long-term homeownership is one of, if not the best investment one can make. Homeownership will always trend long-term because it's the safest path to wealth, and we all need a home.

There you have it…what you need to know about buying a home. Yes, it is complicated and sometimes stressful, but it is worth the time you invested in reading this book to educate and protect yourself.

Start by hiring a great agent to represent you, and do not ever sign anything until you have a thorough understanding of your risks, responsibilities, and your rights. Don't be a lazy buyer!

Most of all, know that before long you will be moving into your new home, and the stress of the home buying process will be long forgotten. You will be putting down roots and becoming part of a new community. Many, many firsts will take place in your new home, and countless memories will be created.

Your home is a real estate investment and an asset that will yield a long-term fortune that is accessible for other investing in whatever your heart desires. Now that you know strategies that will beat the bank's curse of the 'death pledge' to pay outlandish interest fees, you can borrow mortgage money with a sense of confidence and accelerate to your dreams.

Thank You

I would like to thank you from the bottom of my heart for coming along with me on this home buying journey. There are many investing books out there, but you decided to give this one a chance.

If you liked this book, then I need your help!

Please take a moment to leave an honest review of this book. This feedback gives me a good understanding of the kinds of books and topics readers want to read about and it will also give my book more visibility.

Leaving a review takes less than one minute and is much appreciated.

www.ingramcontent.com/pod-product-compliance
Lightning Source LLC
Chambersburg PA
CBHW050447010526
44118CB00013B/1720